When Mommy Has our Baby

written by Rachel A. Cedar
illustrated by Tara J. Hannon

To Eli & Sam

Siblings are the Greatest Gift.

My mommy's tummy is big and round. Our new baby is coming soon! It looks like your mommy is having a baby too.

Will you be a big sister or a big brother?

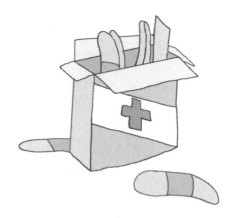

My mommy says she will go to the hospital
when it is time for the baby to come out of her
tummy. The doctor will take good care of her,
just like I take good care of my teddy.

*Where will your mommy go when it is time
for your baby to be born?*

I will miss my mommy while she is gone. It is hard to say goodbye! You may miss your mommy too. My mommy says it is okay to feel sad while we are apart.

Mommy says I will be safe with my
grandma and grandpa. They will be here
to take care of me while mommy and daddy
are at the hospital.

*I bet someone special will take care of you too.
Who will it be?*

I will still go to school, play with my friends and do all the things I normally do while mommy is gone.

What will you do while your mommy is gone having your baby?

Mommy & I made bracelets to wear
while we are apart. If I feel sad, I can
look at my bracelet and remember
how much she loves me.

*You and your mommy can make
something special together too.*

Mommy says a new baby is a reason to celebrate, so we will have a birthday party for our new baby at the hospital. Grandma will help me make a birthday card and bake a cake and cookies for the party.

How will you celebrate your new baby?

I can talk to my mommy on the phone or look at her picture while she is gone. If I feel lonely or miss Mommy, I can tell my grandparents and they will help me feel better.

Be sure to tell your special grown up how you are feeling too.

After the baby is born, Daddy will take me to
visit Mommy & our new baby in the hospital.
I get to wear my special Big Brother tee shirt!

You will be a big sibling soon too!

I feel excited and a little nervous to meet
our new baby, but I'm really happy to see my
mommy again! She gives me a big hug and kiss
and reminds me that I am her special Big Kid.

Our new baby is so tiny! Mommy says the baby loves me very much. I'm not so sure how I feel about her yet and Mommy says that's okay.

It's alright if you feel unsure too.

We sing "Happy Birthday" to our baby and
eat the special cake I made with Grandma.
It's fun to celebrate having a new baby!

I get to snuggle with my mommy and our new baby while Grandma takes our picture all together.

We are now a family of four and soon you will be too!

My mommy and the new baby will stay in the hospital for a few days until the doctor says it okay for them to come home. I will miss them, but I know Mommy always comes back and I will see her soon.

Mommy says she will have to hold the baby a lot when they come home. I may have to wait for her to play with me while she rests and feeds the baby. It will probably be the same with your mommy.

I guess we will both need to be a little patient!

It's going to be hard work being a big sibling. Sometimes it will be fun, but other times, I may not always like having a new baby. I may have to listen to the baby cry, or wait while mommy and daddy take care of her.

Mommy says I can tell her when I'm having a hard time and she will help me feel better.

The new baby is part of our family now. She is with us wherever we go.

She may sleep a lot, but mommy says she will soon learn to smile, sit up, hold toys, eat food, and eventually she will play with me!

Your baby will too!

My mommy's lap will always be big enough to hold me AND our new baby. Mommy and Daddy say they have double the love now, and I bet yours will too. I think that sounds pretty terrific.

What do you think?